to Sainthood

Fr. Thomas Rosica, C.S.B.

NOVALIS

"You Shall Be Holy"

Jesus made his own the call to holiness that God addressed to the people of the first covenant: "You shall be holy; for I the Lord your God am holy" (Leviticus 19:2). He repeated it continually by word and by the example of his life. Especially in the Sermon on the Mount (Matthew 5:1-12), he left to the Church a code of Christian holiness. The Beatitudes found there are a recipe for this holiness.

Holiness is a way of life that involves commitment and activity. It is not a passive endeavour, but rather a continuous choice to deepen our relationship with God and then allow this relationship to guide all our actions in the world. Holiness requires a radical change in mindset and attitude. The acceptance of the call to holiness places God as our final goal in every aspect of our lives.

This fundamental orientation towards God even envelops and sustains our relationship with other human beings. As we are sustained by a life of virtue and fortified by the gifts of the Holy Spirit, God draws us ever closer to himself and to that day when we shall see him face to face in heaven and achieve full union with him.

Friends
of God

Here and now, we can find holiness in our personal experience of putting forth our best efforts in the workplace, patiently raising our children, and building good relationships at home, at school and at work. If we make all of these things a part of our loving response to God, we are on the path of holiness.

A saint is a friend of God who takes the Beatitudes seriously in his or her life. Each of us is called to become God's friend. We grow in friendship with God as we do with others: by being present to God, talking with God and being generous with God. For this purpose, the Church encourages devotion to the saints.

Many people still think
that sainthood is a privilege
reserved only for the chosen
few. Actually, to become a saint
is the task of every Christian –
we could say it's the task
of everyone!

St. Francis of Assisi

St. Marguerite Bourgeoy

At times we may think that
the saints are merely eccentrics
that the Church exalts for
us to imitate – people who
were unrepresentative of and
out of touch with the human
scene. It is certainly true that
all saints are "eccentric" in
its literal sense, for this word
means "outside the centre."
They deviated from the centre,
from usual practice, from the
ordinary ways of doing things,
from the established methods.
Another way of looking at the
saints is to say that they stood
at the radical centre.

We need the example of these holy women and men who had no moderation but only exuberance! They were people with ordinary affections who took God seriously and were therefore free to act with exuberance. Not measured or moderate, the saint's response to God's extravagant love is equally immoderate, marked by fidelity and total commitment. G.K. Chesterton once said of them, "[such] people have exaggerated what the world and the Church have forgotten."

The Roman Catholic Church canonizes certain saints, placing them on a list (canon) of those given the seal of its approval, after long study and a process of discernment. There are far more saints who are not in the canon than are in it; also, many a saint in the canon receives little or no veneration from people today, for it is always the people who finally decide that someone is, for them, a hero.

And if there was ever an age
when young men and women
needed authentic heroes,
it is our age. The Church
understands that saints,
their prayers, their lives, are
for people on earth – that
sainthood, as an earthly honour,
is not coveted by the saints
themselves.

Blessed
John Paul II

The Pope of
Holiness

In the nearly 27 years of his pontificate, Blessed John Paul II gave the Church 1,338 Blesseds and 482 Saints. Karol Wojtyla himself was an extraordinary witness who, through his devotion, heroic efforts, long suffering and death, communicated the powerful message of the Gospel to the men and women of our day.

A great part of the success of his message is due to the fact that he was surrounded by a tremendous cloud of witnesses who stood by him and strengthened him throughout his life. For Blessed John Paul II, the call to holiness excludes no one; it is not the privilege of a spiritual elite.

When the throngs of people
– so many of them the young
men and women who were his
spiritual sons and daughters
– began chanting, "Santo
Subito!" (Make him a saint
soon!) at the end of the Pope's
funeral mass on April 8, 2005,
what were they really saying?
They were crying out that
in Karol Wojtyla, they saw
someone who lived with God
and lived with us.

He was a sinner who experienced God's mercy and forgiveness. He looked at us, loved us, embraced us, healed us and gave us hope. He taught us not to be afraid. He showed us how to live, how to love, how to forgive and how to die. He taught us how to embrace the cross in the most excruciating moments of life, knowing that the cross was not God's final answer.

If the Church has proclaimed
Pope John Paul II "blessed",
it is because he lived with God,
relying totally on God's infinite,
divine mercy, going forward
with God's strength and power,
believing in the impossible,
loving one's enemies and
persecutors, forgiving in the
midst of evil and violence,
hoping beyond all hope,
and leaving the world a
better place.

Blessed John Paul II spoke often to young people about the call to holiness and the vocation to be saints. We remember his message for World Youth Day 2000 in Rome, where his words became the rallying cry for the Jubilee's greatest celebration:

"Young people of every continent, do not be afraid to be the saints of the new millennium! Be contemplative, love prayer; be coherent with your faith and generous in the service of your brothers and sisters, be active members of the Church and builders of peace.

To succeed in this demanding project of life, continue to listen to His Word, draw strength from the Sacraments, especially the Eucharist and Penance. The Lord wants you to be intrepid apostles of his Gospel and builders of a new humanity."

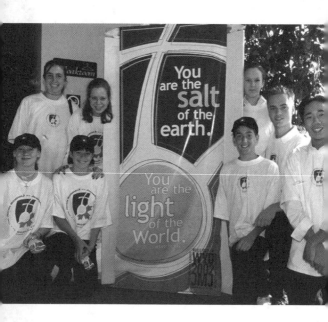

Two years later, at World Youth Day in Canada, John Paul II took up once again the theme of holiness and saints in his message to us:

"Just as salt gives flavor to food and light illumines the darkness, so too holiness gives full meaning to life and makes it reflect God's glory. How many saints, especially young saints, can we count in the Church's history! In their love for God their heroic virtues shone before the world, and so they became models of life which the Church has held up for imitation by all. ...

Through the intercession of this great host of witnesses, may God make you too, dear young people, the saints of the third millennium!"

At the concluding Mass of Toronto's World Youth Day at Downsview Park on July 28, 2002, Pope John Paul issued this stirring challenge:

"And if, in the depths of your hearts, you feel the same call to the priesthood or consecrated life, do not be afraid to follow Christ on the royal road of the Cross! At difficult moments in the Church's life, the pursuit of holiness becomes even more urgent. And holiness is not a question of age; it is a matter of living in the Holy Spirit, just as Kateri Tekakwitha did here in America and so many other young people have done."

Pope Benedict XVI continued the momentum of John Paul's invitations and exhortations to holiness at World Youth Day 2005 in Cologne, Germany. At the opening ceremony on August 18, 2005, Benedict addressed the throng of young people from around the world:

"Dear young people, the Church needs genuine witnesses for the new evangelization: men and women whose lives have been transformed by meeting with Jesus, men and women who are capable of communicating this experience to others. The Church needs saints. All are called to holiness, and holy people alone can renew humanity. Many have gone before us along this path of Gospel heroism, and I urge you to turn often to them to pray for their intercession."

The true defense or apology
of Christian faith, the most
convincing demonstration of
its truth against every denial,
is the saints and the beauty
that their faith has generated.
Today, for faith to grow, we
must encounter the saints
and holy ones and enter into
contact with what is beautiful
and good. This is the vocation
and mission of the Saints and
Blesseds in the Church. Every
crisis that the Church faces,
every crisis that the world
faces, is a crisis of holiness.
Holiness is crucial because it
is the real face of the Church.

St. Isaac Jogues (centre),
one of the Holy Canadian Martyrs

St. Marguerite d'Youville

Saints and Blesseds for Our Times

In the following pages, let us identify some of the great challenges of our times and name some of the holy role models of our Catholic tradition whose lives offer us ways to respond to those challenges: the crisis of fatherhood; upholding the dignity and sacredness of human life; the attacks on freedom of conscience; the care of the poor; the call to holiness for all the baptized; the church's embrace of outcasts; the preservation of bodily and spiritual purity and chastity; and the meaning of authentic friendship.

Fatherhood in Crisis

St. Joseph

Model of Masculinity and Fatherhood

St. Joseph is a great example of masculinity and fatherhood. His paradoxical situation of foster father to Jesus draws attention to the truth about fatherhood. Joseph stood as father to a boy who was his son only in the legal sense. He was keenly aware, as every father should be, that he served as the representative of God the Father.

Joseph understood that he, a mere man conceived and born in sin, had been entrusted to be the head of that family of Nazareth. He neither neglected this authority nor used it for selfish gain. Rather, he exercised his role in perfect humility, in the service of his family. Joseph protected and provided for Jesus and Mary. He named Jesus and taught him how to pray, how to work, how to be a man.

Joseph reveals that fatherhood is more than a mere fact of biological generation. A man is most fully a father when he invests himself in the spiritual and moral formation of his children. Real fathers and real men are those who communicate paternal strength and compassion. They are men of reason in the midst of conflicting passions; men of conviction who always remain open to genuine dialogue about differences; men who ask nothing of others that they wouldn't risk or suffer themselves.

St. Joseph

Joseph is a chaste, faithful, hardworking, simple and just man. He reminds us that a home and a community are not built on power and possessions, but on goodness; not on riches and wealth, but on faith, fidelity, purity and mutual love.

The Dignity
and Sacredness
of Human Life

St. Gianna
Beretta Molla

Lover of Life

Gianna Beretta Molla was an Italian pediatrician and mother. In September 1961, early in her pregnancy with her fourth child, her doctors had diagnosed a serious fibroma in her uterus that required surgery. Gianna had to decide how to proceed. The surgery would save her life, but end her baby's life. She refused to have the operation, and the pregnancy continued.

A few days before the baby was due, Gianna told the doctors her choice: "If you must decide between me and the child, do not hesitate: Choose the child – I insist on it. Save the baby." The doctors did as she asked. Gianna died in 1962 at the age of 39, but her daughter, Gianna Emanuela, lived.

St. Gianna Beretta Moll

Gianna Beretta's action was heroic in that she prepared for it every day of her life. Her final decision for life was the natural flowering and culmination of an extraordinary life of virtue and holiness, selflessness and quiet joy. St. Gianna Molla continues to remind the Church and the world of the need for a consistent ethic of life, from the earliest moments to the final moments of human life.

Beatified in 1994, Gianna was the last saint to be canonized by Blessed John Paul II, ten years later, in 2004.

Freedom of Conscience

Blessed Franz Jägerstätter

Martyr for the Truth

Born in 1907 in Austria, Franz Jägerstätter became one of the outstanding figures of Christian resistance to National Socialism and the Anschluss (annexation of Austria by Germany in March 1938). Franz married and settled down to a typical peasant life, serving his parish as sacristan. In 1940, at the age of 33, he was conscripted into the German armed forces and underwent basic training.

After returning home in 1941
on an exemption as a farmer,
he began examining closely the
religious reasons for refusing
to carry out military service.
In 1943 he reported to his army
base and stated his refusal
to serve. A military court
rejected his assertion that he
could not be both a Nazi and
a Catholic, and condemned
him to death for undermining
military morale. His refusal
to serve in the Nazi army was
not supported by his parish
priest, his bishop or most of his
Catholic friends.

Early on August 9 of the same year, he was taken to the concentration camp at Brandenburg/Havel. At midday he was told his death sentence had been confirmed and would be carried out at 4 p.m. Franz was beheaded, the first of 16 victims, for his refusal to serve in the armies of the Third Reich. Just before his brutal execution he wrote, "I am convinced that it is best that I speak the truth, even if it costs me my life."

This humble man of
St. Radegund offered an
example of how to live the
Christian faith fully and
radically, even when there are
extreme consequences. He is a
shining example in his fidelity
to the claims of his conscience
– an advocate of nonviolence
and peace. On October 26,
2007, in the Cathedral of Linz,
Austria – in the presence of his
94-year-old widow, Franziska,
and his three daughters – Franz
Jägerstätter was beatified as
a martyr, for giving up his life
because of his faith.

St. André Bessette

The Care of
the Poor

St. André
Bessette

Humble Healer

Brother André (born Alfred Bessette), the founder of St. Joseph's Oratory in Montreal, was born into a large Catholic family in 1845 in the village of Saint-Grégoire d'Iberville, Quebec. When he applied to join the Holy Cross Congregation, the superiors decided not to accept him because his poor health would be an impediment to future ministry. Alfred begged the local bishop to intercede, saying, "My only ambition is to serve God in the most humble tasks." The congregation found a place for him among them.

For nearly 40 years, he worked as a porter at the College of Notre-Dame in the Montreal neighbourhood of Côtes-des-Neiges. He urged people who came to him to pray with confidence and perseverance. Word spread quickly when many of those with whom he prayed were healed. But he insisted, "I am nothing … only a tool in the hands of Providence, a lowly instrument at the service of St. Joseph."

Brother André had great faith and a strong devotion to St. Joseph. In 1900, he received permission to raise money for a shrine to his patron. He spent his days seeing sick people who came to him, and his evenings visiting the sick who could not travel to him. Construction on what would become known as St. Joseph's Oratory began in 1914.

St. Joseph's Oratory, Montreal

By the 1920s, the Oratory hosted more than one million pilgrims annually, and hundreds of cures were attributed to his prayers every year. The Oratory is now the largest shrine to St. Joseph in the world. Beatified in 1982 by Blessed John Paul II, Brother André was proclaimed a saint by Pope Benedict XVI in 2010.

The Call to
Holiness for
Lay People

Blessed

Pier Giorgio

Frassati

Man of
the Beatitudes

Pier Giorgio Frassati was born in 1901 into a wealthy, influential family in Turin, Italy. Athletic, full of life, and always surrounded by friends whom he inspired with his life, Pier Giorgio chose not to become a priest or religious, preferring to give witness to the Gospel as a lay person. His friends remember him saying, "To live without faith, without a heritage to defend, without battling constantly for truth, is not to live, but to 'get along'; we must never just 'get along.'"

At the age of 17, he joined the St. Vincent de Paul Society and dedicated much of his spare time to serving the sick and the needy, caring for orphans and assisting demobilized servicemen returning from World War I. Pier Giorgio loved the poor. He gave what he had to help the poor, even using his bus fare for charity and then running home to be on time for meals.

Just before receiving his university degree in mining engineering, he contracted polio, which doctors later speculated he caught from the sick whom he tended. His sacrifice was fulfilled on July 4, 1925. Pier Giorgio Frassati was a young man who combined in a remarkable way political activism, solidarity, work for social justice, piety and devotion, humanity and goodness, holiness and ordinariness, faith and life.

Blessed Pier Giorgio Frassati

God gave Pier Giorgio all the external attributes that could have led him to make the wrong choices: a wealthy and powerful family, good looks and health. But Pier Giorgio listened to the invitation of Christ: "Come, follow me." He anticipated by at least 50 years the Church's understanding and new direction on the role of the laity. Pier Giorgio was beatified by Blessed John Paul II in 1990. He has become one of the principal patrons of World Youth Days.

Caring for Those on the Fringes of Society

St. Marianne Cope

Mother of Outcasts

Sister Marianne Cope was a mother to Molokai lepers. Born Barbara Koob (now officially Cope) on January 23, 1838, and baptized the following day in what is now Hessen, West Germany, Marianne worked as a teacher and hospital administrator. In the 1880s, as superior of her congregation of the Sisters of St. Francis in Syracuse, New York, Mother Marianne responded to the invitation to assist with the care of lepers on the island of Molokai, Hawaii. She loved all whom she served and showed her selfless compassion to those suffering from Hansen's disease (leprosy).

Mother Marianne was about 50 years old when her mission at Molokai began. She spent the last 30 years of her life ministering there, working closely with Father Damien (now St. Damien) and with those who were abandoned on the shores of the island, never to return to their families. After Fr. Damien died, Mother Marianne took charge of the refuge he had built for boys. She died on August 9, 1918, of kidney and heart disease.

She was beatified at the Vatican on May 14, 2005, and was canonized by Pope Benedict on October 21, 2012. People of all religions of the Hawaiian islands still honour and revere St. Damien and St. Marianne, who brought healing to body and soul as they cared for the outcasts of society.

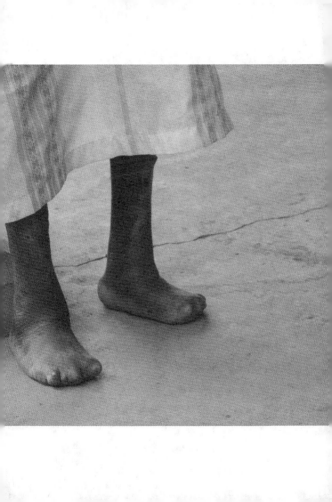

THE LILY
OF THE
MOHAWKS

St. Kateri Tekakwith.

Model of Purity
of Body, Mind
and Heart

St. Kateri
Tekakwitha

Mohawk Mystic

Kateri Tekakwitha, known as the "Lily of the Mohawks," was born to a Christian Algonquin mother and a Mohawk father in 1656 in upstate New York along the Mohawk River. At the age of four, smallpox attacked struck Tekakwitha's village, taking the lives of her parents and baby brother. Smallpox had marked her face and seriously impaired her eyesight, but she survived.

She was adopted by her two aunts and her uncle, also a Mohawk chief. The family abandoned their village and built a new settlement, called Caughnawaga, some five miles away on the north bank of the Mohawk River, which today is in Fonda, New York. Kateri was baptized by a Jesuit missionary in 1676 when she was 20, and became intensely devout. She would deliberately expose herself to the pain of cold and the burning of hot coals, and would pierce her skin with thorns to imitate the suffering of Jesus.

Kateri's family did not accept
her choice to embrace Christ.
After her baptism, she became
the village outcast. Her family
refused her food on Sundays
because she wouldn't work.
Children taunted her and threw
stones. She was threatened
with torture or death if she
did not renounce her religion.
In July 1677, Kateri left her
village and fled more than 200
miles through woods, rivers
and swamps to the Catholic
mission of St. Francis Xavier
at Sault Saint-Louis, near
Montreal.

On March 25, 1679, Kateri made a vow of perpetual virginity, meaning that she would remain unmarried and totally devoted to Christ for the rest of her life. This was unheard of in her culture. Her example of purity and chastity teaches us that the body is our doorway to salvation, and so how we treat it matters. If we cannot say "no," then our "yes" will mean nothing. When we live our sexuality in the proper way, according to our state in life, others will be able to find God through us.

Kateri died during Holy Week on April 17, 1680, at the age of 24. Her last words were "Jesos Konoronkwa" ("Jesus, I love you"). Fifteen minutes after her death, before the eyes of two Jesuits and many Native people, the scars on her face vanished.

In June 1980, Kateri became the first Native American to be beatified. She was canonized as the first Native North American saint in Rome on October 21, 2012.

Discovering
True Friendship

St. Pedro Calúngsod

Good Soldier
of Christ

In a world of instant "friends" on Facebook, many people have lost the meaning of true friendship. A young saint who models authentic, holy friendship and single-minded devotion is the young Filipino migrant St. Pedro Calúngsod.

We know that he was born in 1655, but few details of his early life are available. Pedro was a young lay missionary, catechist and evangelizer, travelling outside his own country to proclaim Christ to other people. Pedro suffered a martyr's death at the age of 17 in modern-day Guam on April 2, 1672, while trying to defend a Jesuit priest, now known as Blessed Diego Luis de San Vitores, from those who hated Christianity.

The attacker hit Calúngsod with a spear and split his skull with a machete. The bodies of the Jesuit and young Pedro were then tied together and thrown into the sea, never to be found. United in life by a deep, holy friendship, the priest and young man endured martyrdom because of the faith that united them.

At his beatification in St. Peter's Basilica on March 5, 2000, Blessed John Paul II praised the young Pedro with these words: "In a spirit of faith, marked by strong Eucharistic and Marian devotion, Pedro undertook the demanding work asked of him and bravely faced the many obstacles and difficulties he met. In the face of imminent danger, Pedro would not forsake Fr. Diego, but as a 'good soldier of Christ' preferred to die at the missionary's side."

On October 21, 2012, during the Synod on the New Evangelization, Pedro Calúngsod became the second Filipino saint (after St. Lorenzo Ruiz, an altar server martyred in Japan while serving in a mission there in 1637). St. Pedro reminds us of the words of Jesus: that there is no greater love than to lay down one's life for one's friends.

The Saints
Are the
Real Portal
of the Church

Lumen Gentium, the Dogmatic Constitution on the Church from the Second Vatican Council, states that the holiness of Christians flows from that of the Church and manifests it. Holiness "is expressed in many ways by the individuals who, each in his own state of life, tend to the perfection of love, thus sanctifying others" (LG 39). In this variety, "one and the same holiness is cultivated by all, who are moved by the Spirit of God … and follow the poor Christ, the humble and crossbearing Christ in order to be worthy of being sharers in his glory" (LG 41).

In his 1990 Encyclical Letter *Redemptoris Missio* ("On the Permanent Validity of the Church's Missionary Mandate"), Blessed John Paul II took up this theme of holiness once again. He wrote,

"The universal call to holiness is closely linked to the *universal call to mission.* Every member of the faithful is called to holiness and to mission. This was the earnest desire of the Council, which hoped to be able "to enlighten all people with the brightness of Christ, which gleams over the face of the Church, by preaching the Gospel to every creature." The Church's missionary spirituality is a journey toward holiness. … What is needed is the encouragement of a new "ardor for holiness" among missionaries and throughout the Christian community.

"Dear brothers and sisters: let us remember the missionary enthusiasm of the first Christian communities. Despite the limited means of travel and communication in those times, the proclamation of the Gospel quickly reached the ends of the earth. And this was the religion of a man who had died on a cross, "a stumbling block to Jews and folly to Gentiles"! (1 Cor 1:23) Underlying this missionary dynamism was the holiness of the first Christians and the first communities." (#90)

Several years before his election to the papacy, Cardinal Joseph Ratzinger told an interviewer, "The only really effective case for Christianity comes down to two arguments, namely, the saints the church has produced and the art which has grown in her womb." As Catholics, we have the blessed privilege of seeking the beauty of holiness and the holiness of beauty.

The lives of the Saints and Blesseds are a great consolation and source of hope and beauty, no matter how difficult the times in which we are living. They offer us a recipe for holiness and model for us lives patterned on the Beatitudes. As Pope Benedict XVI reminded the throngs of young people gathered around him during World Youth Day 2005 in Cologne, Germany, "The saints … are the true reformers. Now I want to express this in an even more radical way: Only from the saints, only from God does true revolution come, the definitive way to change the world."

What attracts us to Christ
and the Church? What keeps
us alive and hopeful in the
Church? Revolutionaries like
Joseph, Gianna Beretta Molla,
Franz Jägerstätter, André
Bessette, Pier Giorgio Frassati,
Marianne Cope, Kateri
Tekakwitha, Pedro Calúngsod,
and "a cloud of witnesses" show
us the way.

The Saints and Blesseds are the real portal of the Church. In the midst of conflict, hostility, suffering and martyrdom, they remained hopeful, strong and joyful. What inspiration they gave to their contemporaries! During times and crises of immense fragmentation and division, they kept their feet firmly planted on earth and their eyes fixed on their heavenly homeland.

They model for us authentically human relationships that begin on earth and lead us into heaven. These holy men and women encourage us by their devotion to Christ, as well as by their courageous zeal and spirit of prayer along the highway to heaven.

They remind us that on this long and at times arduous journey, we are never finished; we are only and always on the way. When we think of holiness in these terms – as a kind of direction, rather than a destination – we have a sense that what unites us with the saints, our fellow travellers, is much deeper than all that sets us apart.

Luciana Frassati. *A Man of the Beatitudes: Pier Giorgio Frassati.* Introduction by Karl Rahner. Ottawa: Novalis, 2000.

http://blessedmariannecope.org

http://www.nps.gov/kala/historyculture/marianne.htm

Fr. Pierre Cholenec, SJ. Catherine *Tekakwitha: Her Life.* Translated by William Lonc, SJ. Montreal: Jesuit Archives, 2002.

Homily by Pope John Paul II at the beatification of Kateri Tekakwitha (1980): http://www.kateritekakwitha.org/kateri/pope.htm

Witness interview with Archbishop Luis Antonio Tagle of Manila on Pedro Calungsod: http://www.youtube.com/watch?feature=player_embedded&v=eu4ooS5H8sA

http://www.pedrocalungsod.org

http://www.pedrocalungsod.net

http://www.youtube.com/watch?v=iK1l_Iy8zAo&feature=youtu.be&noredirect=1

Library and Archives Canada Cataloguing in Publication

BX4655.3.R68 2013   282.092'2   C2013-901728-3

ISBN 978-2-89646-436-4

© 2013 Novalis Publishing Inc.

Layout: Audrey Wells
Cover: Quatre-Quarts and Audrey Wells
Cover photographs: iStockphoto / caracterdesign.
Interior photographs: pp. 2, 13, 14, 37, 45, 52, 78, 85: Plaisted;
pp. 7-8, 104–105: Jupiter Images; p. 28: W.P. Wittman; p. 38:
2010-030, La Bienheureuse Marguerite d'Youville, Sr Flore
Barrette (1897–1984), huile polychrome sur toile, 1959;
p. 50: Used with permission of the Molla Family and Salt and
Light Catholic Media; pp. 58-59, 65: Jocelyn Boutin; p. 60:
Jean-François Rioux; p. 71: Novalis, courtesy of the Frassati
Family; p. 77: iStockphoto; p. 90: public domain.

Published by Novalis

Publishing Office
10 Lower Spadina Avenue, Suite 400
Toronto, Ontario, Canada
M5V 2Z2

Head Office
4475 Frontenac Street
Montréal, Québec, Canada
H2H 2S2

www.novalis.ca

Printed in Canada.

We acknowledge the financial support of the Government
of Canada through the Canada Book Fund for business
development activities.

5 4 3 2 1   17 16 15 14 13